# Collins

# KS2
# Grammar, Punctuation and Spelling

## SATs 10 Minute Tests

Rachel Axten-Higgs

# How to Use this Book

This book contains 17 Key Stage 2 tests. There are 14 Grammar and Punctuation tests and 3 Spelling tests. Each test is designed to be completed in approximately 10 minutes.

Consisting of SATs-style questions in bite-sized chunks, each 10-minute test will help children to prepare for the SATs Grammar, Punctuation and Spelling papers at home.

Clearly laid out questions and easy-to-use answers will help your child become familiar with, and gain confidence in, answering and understanding SATs-style questions.

The tests are all the same level of difficulty, which means they can be carried out in any order and at any time throughout Year 6 to provide invaluable practice for your child.

- Children should work in a quiet environment where they can complete each test undisturbed. They should complete each test in approximately 10 minutes.

- The number of marks available for each question is given on the right-hand side of the test pages, with a total provided at the end of each test.

- For the Spelling tests, you will need to help your child by reading out the words they are required to spell. Instructions are given in the Answers section on page 63.

- Answers and marking guidance are provided for each test.

- A score chart can be found at the back of the book, which your child can use to record their marks and see their progress.

**Acknowledgements**

The author and publisher are grateful to the copyright holders for permission to use quoted materials and images.

Every effort has been made to trace copyright holders and obtain their permission for the use of copyright material. The author and publisher will gladly receive information enabling them to rectify any error or omission in subsequent editions. All facts are correct at time of going to press.

Published by Collins
An imprint of HarperCollins*Publishers*
1 London Bridge Street
London SE1 9GF

ISBN: 9780008335861

Content first published 2019
This edition published 2020
Previously published by Letts

10 9 8 7 6 5 4 3

© HarperCollins*Publishers* Limited 2020

All rights reserved. No part of this publication may be reproduced, stored in a retrieval system, or transmitted, in any form or by any means, electronic, mechanical, photocopying, recording or otherwise, without the prior permission of Collins.

British Library Cataloguing in Publication Data.

A CIP record of this book is available from the British Library.

Author: Rachel Axten-Higgs
Commissioning Editors: Michelle l'Anson and Fiona McGlade
Editor and Project Manager: Katie Galloway
Cover Design: Sarah Duxbury and Kevin Robbins
Inside Concept Design: Ian Wrigley
Text Design and Layout: Jouve India Private Limited
Production: Karen Nulty
Printed by: CPI Group (UK) Ltd, Croydon, CR0 4YY

MIX
Paper from
responsible source
FSC® C007454

FSC
www.fsc.org

This book is produced from independently certified FSC™ paper to ensure responsible forest management.

For more information visit:
www.harpercollins.co.uk/green

# Contents

**1** Which sentence is a **command**?

Tick **one**.

Can I have a pet? ☐

I am having a pet. ☐

My favourite pet is a cat. ☐

Get me a pet cat. ☐

1 mark

**2** Which **word class** is the underlined word in the sentence below?

The girls <u>played</u> football in the rain.

Tick **one**.

adverb ☐

determiner ☐

verb ☐

noun ☐

1 mark

**3** Insert a **colon** in the correct place in the sentence below.

There are two items I must not forget when I go on holiday

my camera and my wallet.

1 mark

**4** What is the name of the **punctuation mark** used between the two main clauses below?

My friend loves playing football; I, however, prefer playing

rugby – especially the scrums.

...........................................................................................................................................................................................

1 mark

**5** Draw a line to match each **prefix** to the correct word so that it makes a new word.

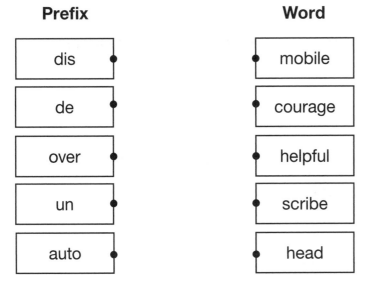

| Prefix | Word |
| --- | --- |
| dis | mobile |
| de | courage |
| over | helpful |
| un | scribe |
| auto | head |

1 mark

**6** Label the boxes with **V (verb)**, **S (subject)** and **O (object)** to show the parts of the sentence.

Oscar played cars.

1 mark

**7** Which sentence is written in Standard English?

Tick **one**.

I played my flute in the school orchestra. ☐

I been to the school hall with my friends. ☐

I seen my friends at the weekend. ☐

I went home and done my music practice. ☐

1 mark

**8** Insert **one** comma in the correct place in the sentence below.

Heading to the shop Harry wandered slowly along the

pavement.

1 mark

**9** Draw a line to match each word to the correct **suffix** to make an **adjective**.

| Word | Suffix |
|------|--------|
| cost | ful |
| colour | ly |
| adore | able |

1 mark

**10** Replace the underlined words in the sentence below with their **expanded forms**.

I'll get some bread but I won't get any sweets as we're going

to the dentist later.

1 mark

6

**11** Which sentence uses **capital letters** correctly?

Tick **one**.

Sam went to london on Saturday morning. ☐

Sam went to London on saturday morning. ☐

Sam went to London on Saturday morning. ☐

sam went to London on Saturday morning. ☐

1 mark

**12** Circle the two words that are **antonyms** in the sentence below.

We had a wonderful holiday at the seaside despite the rain and wind and the awful food at the hotel!

1 mark

**1** Tick the **adverb** in the sentence below.

Tick **one**.

The happy child ran quickly to his young mother.

↑ ↑ ↑ ↑

□ □ □ □

1 mark

**2** What is the grammatical term for the underlined part of the sentence?

The man chased away <u>the dog digging in the new flower bed</u>.

Tick **one**.

an adverbial □

a noun phrase □

a fronted adverbial □

a subordinate clause □

1 mark

**3** Freya wants to know the time the film starts at the cinema.

Write a **question** she could ask to find out.

Remember to punctuate your sentence correctly.

..................................................................................................................................................

..................................................................................................................................................

1 mark

**4** Insert a **semi-colon** in the correct place in the sentence below.

I like eating spaghetti we had spaghetti for lunch today.

1 mark

**5** Replace the underlined word or words in the sentence below with the correct **pronouns**.

At the weekend, Chad visited his aunt and uncle and

<u>his aunt and uncle</u> took <u>Chad</u> to the park.

```
┌──────────┐      ┌──────────┐
│          │      │          │
└──────────┘      └──────────┘
```

1 mark

**6** Which sentence is a statement?

Tick **one**.

Do you like playing football ☐

Do not play football on the grass ☐

You can play football at breaktime ☐

Be careful not to slip over ☐

1 mark

**7** Insert a **subordinating conjunction** to show that the doorbell ringing caused the dog to bark.

_____ the doorbell rang, my dog Dougie barked loudly.

1 mark

**8** Which sentence is punctuated correctly?

Tick **one**.

Anna asked, "Will you help me please" ☐

Anna asked, "will you help me please?" ☐

Anna asked, "Will you help me please?" ☐

Anna asked, "Will you help me please"? ☐

1 mark

**9** Tick one box in each row to show whether the apostrophe is used to show a **contracted form** or to show **possession**.

| Sentence | Apostrophe to show contracted form | Apostrophe to show possession |
|---|---|---|
| I'll see you at school. | | |
| Is this George's coat? | | |
| The pen's on the floor. | | |
| It is the child's bicycle. | | |

1 mark

**10** Circle the two words that show the **tense** in the sentence below.

Ahmed went to the circus and the trapeze show was his favourite part.

1 mark

**11 a)** Write an explanation of the word **synonym**.

...................................................................................................................

...................................................................................................................

1 mark

**b)** Write one word that is a **synonym** of <u>happy</u>.

...................................................................................................................

1 mark

**Total marks** .......... /12

**10 min**

**1** Tick the option that must end with a **question mark**.

Tick **one**.

What we played in PE was fun ☐

Can you guess what we did in PE ☐

Ask me what we did in PE ☐

I will tell you what we played in PE ☐

1 mark

**2** Underline the **subordinate clause** in each sentence below.

Although it was late, Jackie wasn't tired.

If you want some help, you need to ask.

I really love writing, because I am good at it.

1 mark

**3** What does the word <u>Others</u> refer to in the passage below?

Some trees, such as pine trees, keep their leaves in winter.

Others, such as hazel trees, lose their leaves.

Tick **one**.

leaves ☐

trees ☐

hazel trees ☐

pine trees ☐

1 mark

**4** Which sentence is grammatically correct?

Tick **one**.

Next week we went to the bowling alley. ☐

In a month's time, I will be in Cyprus on holiday. ☐

Tomorrow we went to the shops. ☐

Last holiday, we sail on a ferry to France. ☐

1 mark

**5** Which sentence is a **command**?

Tick **one**.

Bring a packed lunch tomorrow. ☐

You could bring a packed lunch. ☐

I am going to bring a packed lunch. ☐

You will need a packed lunch. ☐

1 mark

**6** Which sentence uses the **hyphen** correctly?

Tick **one**.

The bad-tempered shopkeeper-shouted at the boy. ☐

The bad-tempered-shopkeeper shouted at the boy. ☐

The bad-tempered shopkeeper shouted at the boy. ☐

The bad tempered-shopkeeper shouted at the boy. ☐

1 mark

**7** What does the root <u>sign</u> mean in the word family below?

de**sign**        **sign**ature        de**sign**er        **sign**ed

Tick **one**.

Make a design on paper.  ☐

Draw a picture for a person.  ☐

Make a mark for a purpose.  ☐

Sign your name.  ☐

1 mark

**8** Circle the correct **verb form** in each underlined pair to complete the sentences below.

We <u>did/done</u> lots of cycling at the weekend.

When we <u>did/done</u> the decorating, it was hard work!

I have <u>did/done</u> my homework in record time.

1 mark

**9** Circle the **relative pronoun** in the sentence below.

Captain Hook, who is Peter Pan's enemy, lives on a ship.

1 mark

**10** Circle the **possessive determiner** in the passage below.

The guide showed us around the castle. She pointed out

which was its darkest and scariest dungeon.

1 mark

**Total marks** .......... /10

**1** Circle the **possessive pronouns** in the sentence below.

That ball is not yours – it's mine.

1 mark

**2** Which sentence is an **exclamation**?

Tick **one**.

What shall we do tonight ☐

I thought we could play a game ☐

What a great idea ☐

Your idea to play a game is good ☐

1 mark

**3** Insert **one** comma in the correct place in the sentence below.

Waiting for the whistle Maya was in position in the starting block.

1 mark

**4** What is the grammatical term for the underlined words in the sentence below?

My present was <u>a gigantic inflatable Tyrannosaurus Rex toy.</u>

......................................................................................................................

1 mark

**5** Which sentence is the most **formal**?

Tick **one**.

He proposed that his car be used. ☐

He really hopes his car will be OK. ☐

Don't forget to get petrol! ☐

If he's late, we'll take another car. ☐

1 mark

**6** **a)** Write a sentence using the word <u>paints</u> as a **noun**.

Remember to punctuate your answer correctly.

...............................................................................................................................

...............................................................................................................................

1 mark

**b)** Write a sentence using the word <u>paints</u> as a **verb**.

Remember to punctuate your answer correctly.

...............................................................................................................................

...............................................................................................................................

1 mark

**7** Circle the word in the passage that contains an **apostrophe** for **possession**.

It's lunchtime. Let's leave now and we'll reach the park in time for Shaun's lunchtime picnic.

1 mark

**8** Circle the correct **verb form** in each underlined pair to complete the sentences below.

We played with our friends when we <u>were/was</u> at the park.

At the funfair, there <u>was/were</u> many exciting rides.

The car <u>was/were</u> waiting on the driveway.

1 mark

**9** Circle the **conjunction** in each sentence.

We like to go for a walk when it is the weekend.

Although we like getting muddy, it is better when the weather is warm!

My sister doesn't like walking, so she always moans!

1 mark

**10** Explain how the different **prefixes** change the meanings of the two sentences below.

The police officer was <u>untrained.</u>

This means that the police officer ...........................................................................................

..........................................................................................................................................

The police officer was <u>undertrained.</u>

This means that the police officer ...........................................................................................

..........................................................................................................................................

1 mark

**Total marks** ........... /11

**10 min**

**1** Which sentence uses the word <u>light</u> as an **adjective**?

Tick **one**.

A bright light entered his eye. ☐

The light of the sun is bright. ☐

Her eyes were light green. ☐

He lights a fire. ☐

1 mark

**2** Insert a **pair of commas** in the correct place in the sentence below.

My friend who has two geckos let me hold one of them.

1 mark

**3** What is the **word class** of the underlined words in the sentence below?

<u>The</u> boy climbed <u>a</u> tree and picked <u>an</u> apple.

Tick **one**.

adverb ☐

conjunction ☐

verb ☐

determiner ☐

1 mark

**4** Circle the four **prepositions** in the sentence below.

Aboard a boat, you can sail across still water, along narrow channels and between large rocks.

1 mark

**5** Which option completes the sentence in the **past perfect**?

After James _____ his work,

he went to lunch.

Tick **one**.

had finished ☐

has finished ☐

finishes ☐

was finishing ☐

1 mark

**6** **a)** Write an explanation of the word **antonym**.

.................................................................................................................................

.................................................................................................................................

1 mark

**b)** Write one word that is an **antonym** of <u>bold.</u>

.................................................................................................................................

1 mark

**7** Which sentence is a **statement**?

Tick **one.**

You can eat your peas with a spoon ☐

Be careful when you use a fork ☐

Do you prefer a fork or spoon ☐

Do not use your fingers ☐

1 mark

**8** Which sentence must end with a **question mark**?

Tick **one**.

When we will find out the truth, I am not sure ☐

How he didn't fall from that tree is a mystery ☐

Why are we waiting so long for the bus ☐

When it is wet, it makes me grumpy ☐

1 mark

**9** Circle the correct **verb form** in each underlined pair to complete the sentences below.

He isn't/aren't able to come to the party.

Jack says they isn't/aren't coming in from the garden.

She aren't/isn't very good at listening to the rules.

1 mark

**10** Rewrite the two sentences below as one sentence using an appropriate **co-ordinating conjunction**.

Remember to punctuate your answer correctly.

We have time to go to the park. We will have to be back in time for lunch.

...........................................................................................................................

...........................................................................................................................

1 mark

**10 min**

**1** Complete the sentence with an **adjective** formed from the word <u>obey.</u>

The dog was very .............................................. to its master.

1 mark

**2** Tick the sentence that must end with a **question mark**.

Tick **one**.

Why he doesn't listen I will never know ☐

What he is thinking about is unknown to me ☐

When are you going to listen to me ☐

How much he understood is unclear ☐

1 mark

**3** Tick one box in each row to show whether the sentence is written in the **active** or the **passive**.

| Sentence | Active | Passive |
|---|---|---|
| The broken toy was found by the teacher. | | |
| Everyone saw the accident. | | |
| Pippa was frightened by the noise. | | |

1 mark

**4** Underline the **relative clause** in each sentence.

We visited the theatre that showed The Lion King.

My cousin who lives in New Zealand has sent me a letter.

My friend who I play with is on holiday.

1 mark

**5** Insert a **colon** in the correct place in the sentence below.

There are two rides that I have always wanted to go on the teacups and the log flume.

*1 mark*

**6** Label the boxes with **V (verb)**, **S (subject)** and **O (object)** to show the parts of the sentence.

Jasper ate lunch.

☐ ☐ ☐

*1 mark*

**7** Write the name of punctuation that could be used instead of commas in the sentence below.

Eventually, after much crying and wailing, the little boy did what he was asked.

...........................................................................................................................

*1 mark*

**8** Circle each word that should begin with a **capital letter** in the sentence below.

the school at the end of the road is called st mary's and is in the town of weymouth.

*1 mark*

**9** Draw a line to match each word to the correct **suffix** to make an **adjective**.

| Word | Suffix |
|---|---|
| hope | ful |
| love | less |
| wonder | ly |

1 mark

**10** Which sentence is the most **formal**?

Tick **one**.

We love how friendly and kind you are. ☐

Your kindness and generosity are immense. ☐

You have a big heart. ☐

Your kind and friendly words make me happy. ☐

1 mark

Total marks ......... /10

**1** Which sentence uses **capital letters** correctly?

Tick **one**.

We went to France for Ricky's birthday. ☐

we went to France for Ricky's birthday. ☐

We went to france for Ricky's birthday. ☐

We went to france for ricky's birthday. ☐

1 mark

**2** Tick **all** the sentences that contain a **preposition**.

Tim checked his watch before the meeting. ☐

There was excitement among the crowd. ☐

Fiona liked coming first. ☐

The hill towers above the village. ☐

1 mark

**3** Rewrite the underlined verb in the sentence below so that it is in the **present progressive** tense.

I <u>helped</u> my brother to read.

.......................................................................................................................................

1 mark

**4** Kiren wants to know the amount of time the train journey will take.

Write the **question** she could ask to find out.

Remember to punctuate your sentence correctly.

.......................................................................................................................................

.......................................................................................................................................

1 mark

**5** Tick one box in each row to show if the sentence is in the **present progressive** or the **past progressive**.

| Sentence | Present progressive | Past progressive |
|---|---|---|
| Michael was making a model in the classroom this morning. | | |
| Michael's creative skills are developing all the time. | | |
| Michael is hoping to become an architect. | | |

1 mark

**6** What is the grammatical term for the underlined part of the sentence?

<u>Harry fell off his bike</u>, but he didn't hurt himself.

Tick **one.**

an adverbial ☐

a main clause ☐

a noun phrase ☐

a subordinate clause ☐

1 mark

**7** Draw a line to match each **prefix** to the correct word so that it makes a new word. Use each prefix only **once**.

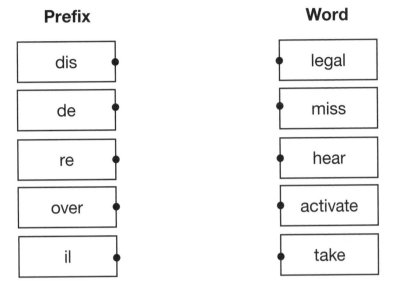

| Prefix | Word |
|--------|------|
| dis | legal |
| de | miss |
| re | hear |
| over | activate |
| il | take |

1 mark

**8** Tick one box in each row to show whether the underlined word is an **adjective** or an **adverb**.

| Sentence | Adjective | Adverb |
|----------|-----------|--------|
| The girl arrived at school <u>early</u>. | | |
| He <u>often</u> worked hard. | | |
| I ran <u>quickly</u> to the cinema. | | |
| The <u>cuddly</u> kitten was cute. | | |

1 mark

**9** Explain how the position of the **apostrophe** changes the meaning of the second sentence.

**1)** What are your sister's favourite clothes?

**2)** What are your sisters' favourite clothes?

.............................................................................................................................

.............................................................................................................................

1 mark

25

**10** Which sentence is closest in meaning to the one below?

My sister has had all her adult teeth for a year now.

Tick **one**.

My sister no longer has her adult teeth. ☐

My sister still has some milk teeth. ☐

My sister has her adult teeth now. ☐

My sister won't have her teeth in 4 years' time. ☐

1 mark

Total marks .......... /10

**10 min**

**1** Circle all the **adverbs** in the sentences below.

Sam happily set off on his journey to fight the huge dragon.

The dragon was sitting quietly in his cave feeling very lonely.

Later, when Sam cautiously approached the dark cave, the

dragon had flown off to find some delicious food.

1 mark

**2** Tick **one** box in each row to show whether the sentence is a **question**, a **statement** or a **command**.

| Sentence | Question | Statement | Command |
|---|---|---|---|
| How many days are there in a year | | | |
| Count the number of days carefully | | | |
| The number of days changes depending on whether it is a leap year | | | |
| Is this year a leap year | | | |

1 mark

**3** Rewrite the sentence below as **direct speech**.

Remember to punctuate your sentence correctly.

I asked her if I could go with her to the park.

I asked, .........................................................................................................................................

.........................................................................................................................................

1 mark

**4** Circle the correct word in each box to complete the sentences in **Standard English**.

We [ was / were ] listening to music in the hideout.

I completed my homework [ good. / well. ]

I [ done / did ] a great impression of a monkey!

1 mark

**5** What is the grammatical term for the underlined words in the sentence below?

The shiny green pine tree is an evergreen.

........................................................................................................

1 mark

**6** What does the root <u>vent</u> mean in the word family below?

in**vent**     ad**vent**     rein**vent**     circum**vent**

Tick **one**.

come ☐

help ☐

clean ☐

love ☐

1 mark

**7** Underline the **adverbial** in the sentence below.

Before singing, Milo drank a glass of water.

1 mark

# Grammar and Punctuation Test 8

**8** Tick one box in each row to show whether the sentence is written in the **active voice** or the **passive voice**.

| Sentence | Active | Passive |
|---|---|---|
| Penguins live in Antarctica. | | |
| Fish are eaten by penguins. | | |
| Usually, penguins huddle to keep warm. | | |

1 mark

**9** Which sentence is punctuated correctly?

Tick **one**.

The children played in the garden – it was very hot and sunny. ☐

The children played in the garden it was – very hot and sunny. ☐

The children – played in the garden it was very hot and sunny. ☐

The children played in the garden it was very – hot and sunny. ☐

1 mark

**10** Which **verb form** completes the sentence?

After Reuben ............................................... his race, he showed his

trophy to the crowd.

Tick **one**.

is winning ☐

had won ☐

has won ☐

was winning ☐

1 mark

**10 min**

**1** Insert a **subordinating conjunction** to show that we ate tea after we had watched a film.

............................................ we ate our tea, we watched a film.

*1 mark*

**2** Rewrite the sentence below, adding a **subordinating clause**.

Remember to punctuate your answer correctly.

The children played in the garden.

................................................................................................................

................................................................................................................

*1 mark*

**3** Insert a **semi-colon** in the correct place in the sentence below.

Come to my house I can't talk to you here in the street.

*1 mark*

**4** Rewrite the verbs in the boxes to complete the sentences with the correct choice of **tense**.

The children went out to play after they ............................................

their snack.

| to finish |

Tiegan usually ............................................ her bike to school and locks

it in the bike shed.      | to ride |

*1 mark*

**5** Complete the sentence below with a **possessive pronoun**.

They are ......................................................... .

1 mark

**6** Circle one verb in each underlined pair to complete the sentences using **Standard English**.

I <u>was/were</u> sad that the holidays were over.

They <u>was/were</u> happy that it was the weekend.

1 mark

**7** Rearrange the words in the statement to make it a **question**.

Use only the given words.

Remember to punctuate your sentence correctly.

Statement:  We are going for a walk.

Question:  ..........................................................................................................

1 mark

**8** Draw a line to match each word to its correct **antonym**.

| Word | Antonym |
|------|---------|
| gently | inconsiderate |
| kindness | false |
| correct | roughly |
| thoughtful | meanness |

1 mark

**9** Underline the **relative clause** in the sentence below.

The new shop which opened last week sells toys.

1 mark

**10** Which sentence is punctuated correctly?

Tick **one**.

Mr Langford the (Chief Executive) gave a speech. ☐

Mr Langford (the Chief Executive gave a speech). ☐

Mr Langford (the Chief Executive) gave a speech. ☐

Mr Langford (the Chief Executive gave a speech.) ☐

1 mark

**Total marks** .......... /10

**10 min**

**1** Insert **full stops** and **capital letters** in the passage below so it is punctuated correctly.

Joshua has always been interested in learning about dinosaurs he has read many books about them and visited museums that contain fossils he would like to become an archaeologist when he is older

1 mark

**2** What is the **subject** of the sentence below?

At the weekend, Charlie is going to a football match with Amir.

Tick **one**.

weekend ☐

Charlie ☐

football ☐

Amir ☐

1 mark

**3** What kind of clause is underlined in the sentence below?

We have a secret handshake <u>when we meet</u>.

......................................................................................................................

1 mark

**4** Tick **one** box to show the correct place for a **colon** in the sentence below.

Jess needed to work hard at her maths homework it

□ ↑    □ ↑    □ ↑    □ ↑

looked daunting.

1 mark

**5** Tick one box in each row to show if the underlined conjunction is a **subordinating conjunction** or a **co-ordinating conjunction**.

| Sentence | Subordinating conjunction | Co-ordinating conjunction |
|---|---|---|
| I love rugby <u>and</u> I love netball. | | |
| <u>Since</u> he has been home, he has been happy. | | |
| I chose a pink bow, <u>because</u> it is my favourite colour. | | |

1 mark

**6** Rewrite the underlined words in the **simple past** tense.

During the car race, the noise <u>does</u> not allow you to speak to

□

the person next to you and the fumes <u>are</u> not very nice.

□

1 mark

**7** Underline the longest possible **noun phrase** in the sentence below.

That film about the meat-eating dinosaurs was scary.

1 mark

**8** Which sentence is written in **Standard English**?

Tick **one**.

I been to lots of parties this year. ☐

At the weekend I seen lots of animals. ☐

I ain't happy about my writing. ☐

I listened carefully to the instructions. ☐

1 mark

**9** Draw a line to match each sentence to its correct **function**.

Use each function box only **once**.

| Sentence | Function |
|---|---|
| I think it will rain this weekend | command |
| Is it going to rain this weekend | exclamation |
| Check the forecast before you leave | question |
| What a lot of rain we have had this year | statement |

1 mark

**10** Which verb completes the sentence so that it uses the **subjunctive form**?

I request that she _____ to the headteacher.

Tick **one**.

write ☐

writes ☐

wrote ☐

is writing ☐

1 mark

**10 min**

**1** Tick one box in each row to show whether the apostrophe is used for a **contracted form** or **possession**.

| Sentence | Apostrophe for a contracted form | Apostrophe for possession |
|---|---|---|
| Where is Jacob's hat? | | |
| Edwin's thirsty. | | |
| The rabbit's in the garden. | | |
| Find Elsie's coat please. | | |

1 mark

**2** Tick the **adverb** in the sentence below.

Tick **one**.

The happy girl ran swiftly through the crowded hall.

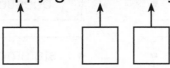 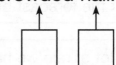

1 mark

**3** Rewrite the sentence below in the **active voice**.

Remember to punctuate your answer correctly.

The precious vase was broken by the black cat.

......................................................................................................................................................

......................................................................................................................................................

1 mark

**4** Tick one box in each row to show if the underlined clause is a **main clause** or a **subordinate clause**.

| Sentence | Main clause | Subordinate clause |
| --- | --- | --- |
| Oscar, <u>who was four years old</u>, loved to play dragons. | | |
| Oscar's mum bought him a catapult <u>so he could launch his dragons in the air</u>. | | |
| <u>Oscar could not play dragons with Edward</u> because Edward was poorly. | | |

1 mark

**5** Circle the two words that show the **tense** in the sentence below.

They climbed the tree in the forest – the climb was very

dangerous.

1 mark

**6** Which two sentences contain a **preposition**?

Tick **two**.

She ran silently. ☐

She fell down the hill. ☐

The cat meowed quietly. ☐

The dog ran past the cat. ☐

1 mark

**7** Insert a **comma** and a **dash** in the correct places in the sentence below.

As usual our class wants to have a dance competition the most

active part of the day.

1 mark

**8** Circle the two words in the sentence below that are **synonyms** of each other.

He was delighted to finish his homework – he knew that if he

worked hard he would complete it in the time given.

1 mark

**9** Which of these sentences is a **command**?

Tick **one**.

After stroking the animals, you will need to wash your hands. ☐

When you have finished stroking the animals, wash your hands. ☐

I want you to wash your hands after stroking the animals. ☐

Here are some rules about stroking the animals. ☐

1 mark

**10** Circle one verb in each underlined pair to complete the sentences using **Standard English**.

He <u>was/were</u> unhappy with his spelling test result.

They <u>was/were</u> going to London for the weekend.

1 mark

**Total marks** .......... /10

## Grammar and Punctuation Test 12

**10 min**

**1** Complete the sentence below with a **noun** formed from the verb <u>decide</u>.

I had a big ............................................ to make.

1 mark

**2** Insert two **hyphens** in the correct places in the sentence below.

The thief left the shop empty handed when the clean shaven

shopkeeper called the police and he heard a siren.

1 mark

**3** Rewrite the sentence below so that it is in the **active voice**.
Remember to punctuate your sentence correctly.

The sweets were eaten by the hungry children.

...................................................................................................................

1 mark

**4** Tick the sentence that must end with a **question mark**.

Tick **one**.

What I need is a paper clip ☐

Ask Mum to help you with that ☐

Where can I find a paper clip ☐

I don't know where to look ☐

1 mark

**5** Which sentence is written in **Standard English**?

Tick **one**.

I done loads of work at my friend's house. ☐

I seen lots of my mates at the park yesterday. ☐

I carried lots of boxes for my teacher. ☐

I been good this week at school. ☐

1 mark

**6** Tick the option that shows how the underlined words in the sentence below are used.

My sister goes to school <u>where my mum works</u>.

Tick **one**.

| | |
|---|---|
| as a preposition phrase | ☐ |
| as a relative clause | ☐ |
| as a main clause | ☐ |
| as a noun phrase | ☐ |

1 mark

**7** Which **word class** is the underlined word in the sentence below?

It was <u>the</u> first day of term.

Tick **one**.

| | |
|---|---|
| adverb | ☐ |
| conjunction | ☐ |
| verb | ☐ |
| determiner | ☐ |

1 mark

**8** Complete the table by adding a **suffix** to each noun to make an **adjective**.

| Noun | Adjective |
|---|---|
| danger | |
| centre | |
| wind | |
| misery | |
| mischief | |

1 mark

**9** Which sentence uses **capital letters** correctly?

Tick **one**.

We are going to a Museum on monday. ☐

There are too many Children in the School. ☐

There is a New Boy starting on Friday. ☐

He is trying to win an Olympic medal. ☐

1 mark

**10** Tick the sentence that uses a **dash** correctly.

Tick **one**.

I like making cakes they are – so good to eat. ☐

I like making cakes they are so – good to eat. ☐

I like making – cakes they are so good to eat. ☐

I like making cakes – they are so good to eat. ☐

1 mark

**10 min**

**1** Which punctuation mark should be used in the place indicated by the arrow?

Simon was excellent at football he was the top scorer for
↑
the club.

Tick **one**.

comma ☐

hyphen ☐

full stop ☐

semi-colon ☐

1 mark

**2** Tick one box in each row to show whether the underlined noun is **singular** or **plural**.

| | Singular | Plural |
|---|---|---|
| The <u>visitors'</u> interest was hooked immediately. | | |
| The <u>mermaid's</u> tail was a beautiful blue. | | |
| Those are the <u>girls'</u> lockers. | | |

1 mark

**3** Tick the sentence that must end with a **question mark**.

Tick **one**.

Tomorrow, I will visit the library ☐

I will ask them to help me choose a book ☐

My favourite books are adventure stories ☐

Which book shall I choose ☐

1 mark

**4** Rewrite the underlined verbs in the sentence below so that they are in the **present progressive** form.

Lauren <u>helps</u> at the market. She <u>hopes</u> to earn money to go

```
┌─────────────┐        ┌─────────────┐
│             │↑       │             │↑
└─────────────┘        └─────────────┘
```

on holiday.

1 mark

**5** Add two **commas** to the sentence below to make it clear that Isaac has four favourite toys.

Isaac's favourite toys are his crane fire engine dinosaurs

and spaceships.

1 mark

**6** Circle the **adverb** in the sentence below.

"Hurrah!" I cried loudly to my little sister.

1 mark

**7** Complete the sentence below with a **noun** formed from the verb <u>educate.</u>

The teacher provided an excellent ................................................ for

her pupils.

1 mark

**8** Tick one box in each row to show whether the underlined clause is a **main clause** or a **subordinate clause**.

| Sentence | Main clause | Subordinate clause |
|---|---|---|
| The ferry, <u>which holds 187 cars</u>, leaves at 9am. | | |
| Although I had worked hard, <u>I still wanted to play football after school</u>. | | |
| <u>We will be happy</u> if we win the match. | | |

1 mark

**9** Circle one verb in each underlined pair to complete the sentences using **Standard English.**

You <u>was/were</u> unlucky to not win a prize.

They <u>was/were</u> all winners of the school trophy.

1 mark

**10** Complete the sentence with an appropriate **subordinating conjunction.**

Felix went outside ......................................................... the sun was shining.

1 mark

**1** Replace the underlined word or words in the sentence below with the correct **pronouns**.

On Saturday, Hattie played in a concert and <u>the concert</u> made <u>Hattie</u> very happy.

1 mark

**2** Which sentence must **not** end with an **exclamation mark**?

Tick **one**.

What a perfect day ☐

I absolutely love chocolate ☐

Was it white chocolate ☐

How delicious ☐

1 mark

**3** What is the **word class** of the underlined word in the sentence below?

<u>Before</u> we went to bed, we had to finish our homework.

Tick **one**.

noun ☐

conjunction ☐

verb ☐

determiner ☐

1 mark

**4** Which sentence contains a **relative clause**?

Tick **one**.

The girl who was on the bike was wearing pink. ☐

The team is practising for their match. ☐

Callum said he wanted to learn to waterski. ☐

They have free time so they like to play football. ☐

1 mark

**5** Write a **command** which could be the first step in the instructions for riding a bike.

Remember to punctuate your answer correctly.

.................................................................................................................................

1 mark

**6** Which sentence is the most **formal**?

Tick **one**.

It's nice to raise money for charity. ☐

Raising money for charity is very worthwhile. ☐

Helping to raise money for charity is really cool. ☐

You should try to raise loads of money for charity. ☐

1 mark

**7** Circle the **adverb** in the sentences below.

Zayna collected cuddly toys. Her favourite was a panda

called Boom Boom because she had excitedly bought

it with her own money.

1 mark

**8** Which verb is a **synonym** of the verb <u>help</u>?

Tick **one**.

hope ☐

assist ☐

change ☐

complete ☐

1 mark

**9** Which sentence shows that you are **most likely** to be here tomorrow?

Tick **one**.

I could be here tomorrow. ☐

I might be away tomorrow. ☐

I shall be away tomorrow. ☐

I will be here tomorrow. ☐

1 mark

**10** The prefix <u>dis-</u> can be added to the root word <u>miss</u> to make the word **dismiss.**

Tick the meaning of the word **dismiss.**

Tick **one**.

to miss out ☐

to send away ☐

to play with ☐

to meddle ☐

1 mark

**10 min**

**1** An ................................................................ closed the road.     1 mark

**2** He had to ................................................................ with the reporter.     1 mark

**3** They ................................................................ announced the winner.     1 mark

**4** I like doing experiments in ................................................................ lessons.     1 mark

**5** They had a ................................................................ wait for their lunch.     1 mark

**6** I had no ................................................................ who had made the mess.     1 mark

**7** The applause at the end was ................................................................     1 mark

**8** The children found ................................................................ at the end of the hunt.     1 mark

**Total marks** ........../8

**1** The ............................................................ to stop the race was unpopular.  
*1 mark*

**2** James was always ............................................................ his bag.  
*1 mark*

**3** There was a lot of ............................................................ to do for the show.  
*1 mark*

**4** The ............................................................ was cooking lunch for the group.  
*1 mark*

**5** It is ............................................................ that you listen to instructions.  
*1 mark*

**6** They ............................................................ to take an umbrella with them.  
*1 mark*

**7** It is a good idea to be ............................................................ when you try things for the first time.  
*1 mark*

**8** The bride walked down the ............................................................ on her wedding day.  
*1 mark*

**10 min**

**1** It was a ........................................................................ that needed to be solved.

1 mark

**2** It is fun to be ........................................................................ and adventurous!

1 mark

**3** The ........................................................................ played to a full concert hall.

1 mark

**4** All the children were able to join in with the ........................................................................
of the song.

1 mark

**5** The football club was top of the ........................................................................

1 mark

**6** The magician was able to ........................................................................ his audience.

1 mark

**7** The goods were ........................................................................ from the lorry
to the ship.

1 mark

**8** The police officer was ........................................................................ to make an
arrest in case it was the wrong person.

1 mark

**Total marks** .......... /8

# Answers

## Grammar and Punctuation Test Answers

| Question | Answer | Marks |
|---|---|---|
| **Test 1** | | |
| 1 | Award 1 mark for **Get me a pet cat.** ✓ | 1 |
| 2 | Award 1 mark for **verb** ✓ | 1 |
| 3 | Award 1 mark for putting the colon in the correct place as shown:<br>There are two items I must not forget when I go on holiday**:** my camera and my wallet. | 1 |
| 4 | Award 1 mark for **semi-colon**<br>Spelling does not need to be correct to award the mark. | 1 |
| 5 | Award 1 mark for all five correct as shown:<br><br>**Prefix**      **Word**<br>dis             mobile<br>de              courage<br>over          helpful<br>un              scribe<br>auto         head | 1 |
| 6 | Award 1 mark for all three letters written in the correct boxes as shown:<br>Oscar played cars.<br><br>S   V   O | 1 |
| 7 | Award 1 mark for **I played my flute in the school orchestra.** ✓ | 1 |
| 8 | Award 1 mark for putting the comma in the correct place as shown:<br>Heading to the shop**,** Harry wandered slowly along the pavement. | 1 |
| 9 | Award 1 mark for all three correct as shown:<br><br>**Word**      **Suffix**<br>cost          ful<br>colour      ly<br>adore       able | 1 |
| 10 | Award 1 mark for all three correctly written expanded forms:<br>I will<br>will not<br>we are | 1 |
| 11 | Award 1 mark for **Sam went to London on Saturday morning.** ✓ | 1 |
| 12 | Award 1 mark for circling the correct two words as shown:<br>We had a (wonderful) holiday at the seaside despite the rain and wind and the (awful) food at the hotel! | 1 |
| **Test 2** | | |
| 1 | Award 1 mark for ticking the correct box as shown:<br>The happy child ran quickly to his young mother.<br><br>✓ | 1 |
| 2 | Award 1 mark for **a noun phrase** ✓ | 1 |

# Answers

| Question | Answer | Marks |
|---|---|---|
| 3 | Award 1 mark for a grammatically correct and accurately punctuated question, e.g.<br>• *What time is the film starting?*<br>• *What time does the film at the cinema start?*<br>• *What time does the film start?*<br>Also accept a correctly constructed and punctuated question that is within inverted commas, e.g.<br>• *"What time does the film start?"*<br>Do not accept a sentence where the question is within a statement, e.g.<br>• *Freya asked, "What time does the film start?"* | 1 |
| 4 | Award 1 mark for putting the semi-colon in the correct place as shown:<br>I like eating spaghetti; we had spaghetti for lunch today. | 1 |
| 5 | Award 1 mark for both words correctly written in the boxes:<br>At the weekend, Chad visited his aunt and uncle and <u>his aunt and uncle</u> took <u>Chad</u> to the park.<br><br>they      him | 1 |
| 6 | Award 1 mark for **You can play football at breaktime** ✓ | 1 |
| 7 | Award 1 mark for **When**<br>It does not need to have a capital letter for the mark to be awarded.<br>Also accept *Because* or *As* | 1 |
| 8 | Award 1 mark for **Anna asked, "Will you help me please?"** ✓ | 1 |
| 9 | Award 1 mark for all four ticks correctly placed as shown: | 1 |

| Sentence | Apostrophe to show contracted form | Apostrophe to show possession |
|---|---|---|
| I'll see you at school. | ✓ | |
| Is this George's coat? | | ✓ |
| The pen's on the floor. | ✓ | |
| It is the child's bicycle. | | ✓ |

| Question | Answer | Marks |
|---|---|---|
| 10 | Award 1 mark for circling the correct two words as shown:<br>Ahmed (went) to the circus and the trapeze show (was) his favourite part. | 1 |
| 11 | **a)** Award 1 mark for a correct explanation of the word **synonym,** e.g.<br>• *They are words or phrases that mean the same as each other.*<br>Accept answers with spelling errors if the explanation is correct. | 1 |
| | **b)** Award 1 mark for a word that is a true synonym of the word <u>happy</u>, e.g.<br>• *content*<br>• *pleased*<br>• *joyful* | 1 |
| **Test 3** | | |
| 1 | Award 1 mark for **Can you guess what we did in PE** ✓ | 1 |
| 2 | Award 1 mark for underlining all three subordinate clauses correctly as shown:<br><u>Although it was late</u>, Jackie wasn't tired.<br><u>If you want some help</u>, you need to ask.<br>I really love writing, <u>because I am good at it</u>. | 1 |
| 3 | Award 1 mark for **trees** ✓ | 1 |
| 4 | Award 1 mark for **In a month's time, I will be in Cyprus on holiday.** ✓ | 1 |

# Answers

| Question | Answer | Marks |
|---|---|---|
| 5 | Award 1 mark for **Bring a packed lunch tomorrow.** ✓ | 1 |
| 6 | Award 1 mark for **The bad-tempered shopkeeper shouted at the boy.** ✓ | 1 |
| 7 | Award 1 mark for **Make a mark for a purpose.** ✓ | 1 |
| 8 | Award 1 mark for circling the three correct words as shown:<br>We (did)/done lots of cycling at the weekend.<br>When we (did)/done the decorating, it was hard work!<br>I have did /(done) my homework in record time. | 1 |
| 9 | Award 1 mark for circling the correct word as shown:<br>Captain Hook, (who) is Peter Pan's enemy, lives on a ship. | 1 |
| 10 | Award 1 mark for circling the correct word as shown:<br>The guide showed us around the castle. She pointed out which was (its) darkest and scariest dungeon. | 1 |
| **Test 4** | | |
| 1 | Award 1 mark for circling both possessive pronouns as shown:<br>That ball is not (yours) – it's (mine). | 1 |
| 2 | Award 1 mark for **What a great idea** ✓ | 1 |
| 3 | Award 1 mark for putting the comma in the correct place as shown:<br>Waiting for the whistle, Maya was in position in the starting block. | 1 |
| 4 | Award 1 mark for **noun phrase** or **expanded noun phrase** | 1 |
| 5 | Award 1 mark for **He proposed that his car be used.** ✓ | 1 |
| 6 | **a)** Award 1 mark for a sentence using 'paints' as a noun, e.g.<br>• The paints are kept in the shed.<br>• There were lots of paints in the classroom.<br><br>**b)** Award 1 mark for a sentence using 'paints' as a verb, e.g.<br>• He paints wonderful pictures.<br>• She paints the rooms in her house. | 1<br><br><br><br>1 |
| 7 | Award 1 mark for circling the correct word as shown:<br>It's lunchtime. Let's leave now and we'll reach the park in time for (Shaun's) lunchtime picnic. | 1 |
| 8 | Award 1 mark for circling the three correct options as shown:<br>We played with our friends when we (were)/was at the park.<br>At the funfair, there was/(were) many exciting rides.<br>The car (was)/were waiting on the driveway. | 1 |
| 9 | Award 1 mark for circling the three conjunctions as shown:<br>We like to go for a walk (when) it is the weekend.<br>(Although) we like getting muddy, it is better when the weather is warm!<br>My sister doesn't like walking, (so) she always moans! | 1 |
| 10 | Award 1 mark for both parts correct:<br>Explanations should say that:<br>• untrained = has had no training at all<br>• undertrained = has had some training, but not enough | 1 |
| **Test 5** | | |
| 1 | Award 1 mark for **Her eyes were light green.** ✓ | 1 |
| 2 | Award 1 mark for putting the commas in the correct places as shown:<br>My friend, who has two geckos, let me hold one of them. | 1 |
| 3 | Award 1 mark for **determiner** ✓ | 1 |

# Answers

| Question | Answer | Marks |
|---|---|---|
| 4 | Award 1 mark for circling all four prepositions as shown:<br>(Aboard) a boat, you can sail (across) still water, (along) narrow channels and (between) large rocks. | 1 |
| 5 | Award 1 mark for **had finished** ✓ | 1 |
| 6 | **a)** Award 1 mark for a correct explanation of the word antonym, e.g.<br>• *A word opposite in meaning to another.*<br><br>Accept answers with spelling errors if the explanation is correct.<br><br>**b)** Award 1 mark for a word that is a true antonym of the word *bold*, e.g.<br>• *afraid*<br>• *timid*<br>• *cowardly*<br>• *unadventurous*<br>• *feint* | 1<br><br>1 |
| 7 | Award 1 mark for **You can eat your peas with a spoon** ✓ | 1 |
| 8 | Award 1 mark for **Why are we waiting so long for the bus** ✓ | 1 |
| 9 | Award 1 mark for circling all three correct options as shown:<br>He (isn't)/aren't able to come to the party.<br>Jack says they isn't /(aren't) coming in from the garden.<br>She aren't/(isn't) very good at listening to the rules. | 1 |
| 10 | Award 1 mark for one sentence written with a co-ordinating conjunction such as **but**, **yet**, e.g.<br>• We have time to go to the park **but** we will have to be back in time for lunch. | 1 |

**Test 6**

| Question | Answer | Marks |
|---|---|---|
| 1 | Award 1 mark for **obedient**<br>Accept spelling errors if the word is identifiable. | 1 |
| 2 | Award 1 mark for **When are you going to listen to me** ✓ | 1 |
| 3 | Award 1 mark for all three ticks correctly placed as shown: | 1 |

| Sentence | Active | Passive |
|---|---|---|
| The broken toy was found by the teacher. | | ✓ |
| Everyone saw the accident. | ✓ | |
| Pippa was frightened by the noise. | | ✓ |

| Question | Answer | Marks |
|---|---|---|
| 4 | Award 1 mark for underlining all three relative clauses correctly as shown:<br>We visited the theatre <u>that showed The Lion King</u>.<br>My cousin <u>who lives in New Zealand</u> has sent me a letter.<br>My friend <u>who I play with</u> is on holiday. | 1 |
| 5 | Award 1 mark for putting the colon in the correct place as shown:<br>There are two rides that I have always wanted to go on: the teacups and the log flume. | 1 |
| 6 | Award 1 mark for all three letters written in the correct boxes as shown:<br>Jasper ate lunch.<br>S V O | 1 |
| 7 | Award 1 mark for **brackets** or **dashes** | 1 |
| 8 | Award 1 mark for circling the four correct words as shown:<br>(the) school at the end of the road is called (st) (mary's) and is in the town of (weymouth.) | 1 |

# Answers

| Question | Answer | Marks |
|---|---|---|
| 9 | Award 1 mark for all three correct as shown:<br><br>**Word**      **Suffix**<br>hope        ful<br>love        less<br>wonder      ly<br><br>Also accept 'hopeful' and 'wonderless'. | 1 |
| 10 | Award 1 mark for **Your kindness and generosity are immense.** ✓ | 1 |

**Test 7**

| Question | Answer | Marks |
|---|---|---|
| 1 | Award 1 mark for **We went to France for Ricky's birthday.** ✓ | 1 |
| 2 | Award 1 mark for all three of the following sentences ticked:<br>**Tim checked his watch before the meeting.** ✓<br>**There was excitement among the crowd.** ✓<br>**The hill towers above the village.** ✓ | 1 |
| 3 | Award 1 mark for **I am helping my brother to read.** | 1 |
| 4 | Award 1 mark for a grammatically correct and accurately punctuated question, e.g.<br>• *How long will the train journey last?*<br>• *What amount of time will the train journey take?*<br><br>Also accept a correctly constructed and punctuated question that is within inverted commas, e.g.<br>• *"How long will the train journey last?"*<br><br>Do not accept a sentence where the question is within a statement, e.g.<br>• *Kiren asked, "How long will the train journey last?"* | 1 |
| 5 | Award 1 mark for all three ticks correctly placed as shown: | 1 |

| Sentence | Present progressive | Past progressive |
|---|---|---|
| Michael was making a model in the classroom this morning. | | ✓ |
| Michael's creative skills are developing all the time. | ✓ | |
| Michael is hoping to become an architect. | ✓ | |

| Question | Answer | Marks |
|---|---|---|
| 6 | Award 1 mark for **a main clause** ✓ | 1 |
| 7 | Award 1 mark for all five correct as shown:<br><br>**Prefix**      **Word**<br>dis        legal<br>de        miss<br>re        hear<br>over      activate<br>il        take | 1 |
| 8 | Award 1 mark for all four ticks correctly placed as shown: | 1 |

| Sentence | Adjective | Adverb |
|---|---|---|
| The girl arrived at school <u>early</u>. | | ✓ |
| He <u>often</u> worked hard. | | ✓ |
| I ran <u>quickly</u> to the cinema. | | ✓ |
| The <u>cuddly</u> kitten was cute. | ✓ | |

# Answers

| Question | Answer | Marks |
|---|---|---|
| 9 | Award 1 mark for an explanation that says:<br>• The first sentence refers to one sister whereas the second sentence refers to more than one sister. | 1 |
| 10 | Award 1 mark for **My sister has her adult teeth now.** ✓ | 1 |

**Test 8**

| Question | Answer | Marks |
|---|---|---|
| 1 | Award 1 mark for circling all five adverbs as shown:<br>Sam (happily) set off on his journey to fight the huge dragon.<br>The dragon was sitting (quietly) in his cave feeling very (lonely.)<br>(Later,) when Sam (cautiously) approached the dark cave, the dragon had flown off to find some delicious food. | 1 |
| 2 | Award 1 mark for all four ticks correctly placed as shown: | 1 |

| Sentence | Question | Statement | Command |
|---|---|---|---|
| How many days are there in a year | ✓ | | |
| Count the number of days carefully | | | ✓ |
| The number of days changes depending on whether it is a leap year | | ✓ | |
| Is this year a leap year | ✓ | | |

| Question | Answer | Marks |
|---|---|---|
| 3 | Award 1 mark for a grammatically correct and accurately punctuated question, e.g.<br>• I asked, "Can I go to the park with you?"<br>Accept slight variations as long as the key information is there and it is in question form as direct speech. | 1 |
| 4 | Award 1 mark for circling the three correct options as shown:<br>was /(were); good /(well); done /(did) | 1 |
| 5 | Award 1 mark for **Expanded noun phrase** | 1 |
| 6 | Award 1 mark for **come** ✓ | 1 |
| 7 | Award 1 mark for underling the adverbial as shown:<br>Before singing, Milo drank a glass of water. | 1 |
| 8 | Award 1 mark for all three ticks correctly placed as shown: | 1 |

| Sentence | Active | Passive |
|---|---|---|
| Penguins live in Antarctica. | ✓ | |
| Fish are eaten by penguins. | | ✓ |
| Usually, penguins huddle to keep warm. | ✓ | |

| Question | Answer | Marks |
|---|---|---|
| 9 | Award 1 mark for **The children played in the garden – it was very hot and sunny.** ✓ | 1 |
| 10 | Award 1 mark for **had won** ✓ | 1 |

**Test 9**

| Question | Answer | Marks |
|---|---|---|
| 1 | Award 1 mark for the sentence written with a suitable subordinating conjunction, such as **before**, e.g.<br>• **Before** we ate our tea, we watched a film. | 1 |

# Answers

| Question | Answer | Marks |
|---|---|---|
| 2 | Award 1 mark for a sentence written with a suitable subordinating clause, e.g.<br>• The children played in the garden, **because the weather was nice.**<br>• The children played in the garden, **before having lunch.**<br>• **When the rain stopped**, the children played in the garden. | 1 |
| 3 | Award 1 mark for putting the semi-colon in the correct place as shown:<br>Come to my house**;** I can't talk to you here in the street. | 1 |
| 4 | Award 1 mark for both correct as shown:<br>**had finished**<br>**rides** | 1 |
| 5 | Award 1 mark for a suitable possessive pronoun, e.g.<br>• **his/hers**<br>• **theirs**<br>• **mine/ours**<br>• **yours** | 1 |
| 6 | Award 1 mark for circling both correct options as shown:<br>I (was) /were sad that the holidays were over.<br>They was/ (were) happy that it was the weekend. | 1 |
| 7 | Award 1 mark for **Are we going for a walk?**<br>Capital letters and punctuation MUST be correct. No additional words must be added. | 1 |
| 8 | Award 1 mark for all four correct as shown:<br>**Word**  **Antonym**<br>gently — roughly<br>kindness — meanness<br>correct — false<br>thoughtful — inconsiderate | 1 |
| 9 | Award 1 mark for underlining the relative clause, as shown:<br>The new shop <u>which opened last week</u> sells toys. | 1 |
| 10 | Award 1 mark for **Mr Langford (the Chief Executive) gave a speech.** ✓ | 1 |
| **Test 10** | | |
| 1 | Award 1 mark for using full stops and capital letters correctly as shown:<br>Joshua has always been interested in learning about dinosaurs. **H**e has read many books about them and visited museums that contain fossils. **H**e would like to become an archaeologist when he is older**.** | 1 |
| 2 | Award 1 mark for **Charlie** ✓ | 1 |
| 3 | Award 1 mark for **Subordinate clause** | 1 |
| 4 | Award 1 mark for ticking the correct box as shown:<br>Jess needed to work hard at her maths homework ↑ it looked daunting.<br>✓ | 1 |
| 5 | Award 1 mark for all three ticks correctly placed as shown: | 1 |

| Sentence | Subordinating conjunction | Co-ordinating conjunction |
|---|---|---|
| I love rugby <u>and</u> I love netball. | | ✓ |
| <u>Since</u> he has been home, he has been happy. | ✓ | |
| I chose a pink bow, <u>because</u> it is my favourite colour. | ✓ | |

# Answers

| Question | Answer | Marks |
|---|---|---|
| 6 | Award 1 mark for writing the verbs in the simple past tense as shown:<br>During the car race, the noise <u>does</u> not allow you to speak to the person next to you and the fumes <u>are</u> not very nice.<br>were ↑ (under *does* = did), (under *are* = were) | 1 |
| 7 | Award 1 mark for underlining the noun phrase as shown:<br><u>That film about the meat-eating dinosaurs</u> was scary. | 1 |
| 8 | Award 1 mark for **I listened carefully to the instructions.** ✓ | 1 |
| 9 | Award 1 mark for all four correct as shown:<br>I think it will rain this weekend — command<br>Is it going to rain this weekend — exclamation<br>Check the forecast before you leave — question<br>What a lot of rain we have had this year — statement | 1 |
| 10 | Award 1 mark for **write** ✓ | 1 |

## Test 11

| Question | Answer | Marks |
|---|---|---|
| 1 | Award 1 mark for all four ticks correctly placed as shown: | 1 |

| Sentence | Apostrophe for a contracted form | Apostrophe for possession |
|---|---|---|
| Where is Jacob's hat? | | ✓ |
| Edwin's thirsty. | ✓ | |
| The rabbit's in the garden. | ✓ | |
| Find Elsie's coat please. | | ✓ |

| Question | Answer | Marks |
|---|---|---|
| 2 | Award 1 mark for ticking the correct box as shown:<br>The happy girl ran swiftly through the crowded hall.<br>↑<br>✓ | 1 |
| 3 | Award 1 mark for a suitable version of the sentence in the active voice, e.g.<br>• The black cat broke the precious vase. | 1 |
| 4 | Award 1 mark for all four ticks correctly placed as shown: | 1 |

| Sentence | Main clause | Subordinate clause |
|---|---|---|
| Oscar, <u>who was four years old</u>, loved to play dragons. | | ✓ |
| Oscar's mum bought him a catapult <u>so he could launch his dragons in the air</u>. | | ✓ |
| <u>Oscar could not play dragons with Edward</u> because Edward was poorly. | ✓ | |

| Question | Answer | Marks |
|---|---|---|
| 5 | Award 1 mark for circling both words that show tense as shown:<br>They (climbed) the tree in the forest – the climb (was) very dangerous. | 1 |
| 6 | Award 1 mark for **She fell down the hill** ✓ and **The dog ran past the cat.** ✓ | 1 |
| 7 | Award 1 mark for both punctuation marks added correctly as shown:<br>As usual**,** our class wants to have a dance competition – the most active part of the day. | 1 |

# Answers

| Question | Answer | Marks |
|---|---|---|
| 8 | Award 1 mark for circling the two correct words as shown:<br>He was delighted to (finish) his homework – he knew that if he worked hard he would (complete) it in the time given. | 1 |
| 9 | Award 1 mark for **When you have finished stroking the animals, wash your hands.** ✓ | 1 |
| 10 | Award 1 mark for circling the two correct words as shown:<br>He (was) /were unhappy with his spelling test result.<br>They **was /** (were) going to London for the weekend. | 1 |

### Test 12

| Question | Answer | Marks |
|---|---|---|
| 1 | Award 1 mark for **decision** | 1 |
| 2 | Award 1 mark for putting hyphens in the correct places as shown:<br>The thief left the shop empty-handed when the clean-shaven shopkeeper called the police and he heard a siren. | 1 |
| 3 | Award 1 mark for a suitable sentence written in the active voice, e.g.<br>• The hungry children ate the sweets. | 1 |
| 4 | Award 1 mark for **Where can I find a paper clip** ✓ | 1 |
| 5 | Award 1 mark for **I carried lots of boxes for my teacher.** ✓ | 1 |
| 6 | Award 1 mark for **as a relative clause** ✓ | 1 |
| 7 | Award 1 mark for **determiner** ✓ | 1 |
| 8 | Award 1 mark for all five adjectives correct as shown:<br><br>| Noun | Adjective |<br>|---|---|<br>| danger | **dangerous** |<br>| centre | **central** |<br>| wind | **windy** |<br>| misery | **miserable** |<br>| mischief | **mischievous** |<br><br>Accept spelling errors if the words are identifiable. | 1 |
| 9 | Award 1 mark for **He is trying to win an Olympic medal.** ✓ | 1 |
| 10 | Award 1 mark for **I like making cakes – they are so good to eat.** ✓ | 1 |

### Test 13

| Question | Answer | Marks |
|---|---|---|
| 1 | Award 1 mark for **semi-colon** ✓ | 1 |
| 2 | Award 1 mark for all three ticks correctly placed as shown:<br><br>| | Singular | Plural |<br>|---|---|---|<br>| The visitors' interest was hooked immediately. | | ✓ |<br>| The mermaid's tail was a beautiful blue. | ✓ | |<br>| Those are the girls' lockers. | | ✓ | | 1 |
| 3 | Award 1 mark for **Which book shall I choose** ✓ | 1 |

# Answers

| Question | Answer | Marks |
|---|---|---|
| 4 | Award 1 mark for writing the present progressive forms correctly as shown: Lauren <u>helps</u> at the market. She <u>hopes</u> to earn money to go on holiday. <br> is helping     is hoping | 1 |
| 5 | Award 1 mark for putting two commas in the correct place as shown: Isaac's favourite toys are his crane**,** fire engine**,** dinosaurs and spaceships. | 1 |
| 6 | Award 1 mark for circling the adverb as shown: "Hurrah!" I cried (loudly) to my little sister. | 1 |
| 7 | Award 1 mark for **education** | 1 |
| 8 | Award 1 mark for all three ticks correctly placed as shown: | 1 |

| Sentence | Main clause | Subordinate clause |
|---|---|---|
| The ferry, <u>which holds 187 cars</u>, leaves at 9am. | | ✓ |
| Although I had worked hard, <u>I still wanted to play football after school</u>. | ✓ | |
| <u>We will be happy</u> if we win the match. | ✓ | |

| Question | Answer | Marks |
|---|---|---|
| 9 | Award 1 mark for circling the two correct words as shown: You <u>was</u>/(were) unlucky to not win a prize. They <u>was</u>/(were) all winners of the school trophy. | 1 |
| 10 | Award 1 mark for the sentence written with a suitable subordinating conjunction, such as **because, when, as, whenever**, e.g. <br> • Felix went outside **because** the sun was shining. | 1 |

## Test 14

| Question | Answer | Marks |
|---|---|---|
| 1 | Award 1 mark for two suitable pronouns used as shown: On Saturday, Hattie played in a concert and <u>the concert</u> made <u>Hattie</u> very happy. <br> it     her | 1 |
| 2 | Award 1 mark for **Was it white chocolate** ✓ | 1 |
| 3 | Award 1 mark for **conjunction** ✓ | 1 |
| 4 | Award 1 mark for **The girl who was on the bike was wearing pink.** ✓ | 1 |
| 5 | Award 1 mark for a grammatically correct and accurately punctuated command, e.g. <br> • *Put on your helmet.* <br> • *Hold your bike steady.* <br> • *Carefully get on your bike.* | 1 |
| 6 | Award 1 mark for **Raising money for charity is very worthwhile.** ✓ | 1 |
| 7 | Award 1 mark for circling the adverb as shown: Zayna collected cuddly toys. Her favourite was a panda called Boom Boom because she had (excitedly) bought it with her own money. | 1 |
| 8 | Award 1 mark for **assist** ✓ | 1 |
| 9 | Award 1 mark for **I will be here tomorrow.** ✓ | 1 |
| 10 | Award 1 mark for **to send away** ✓ | 1 |

# Answers

## Spelling Test Answers

You will need to help your child to carry out the spelling tests.

Read the following instruction out to your child:

*I am going to read the sentences to you. Each sentence has a word missing. Listen carefully to the missing word and fill in the answer space, making sure that you spell the missing word correctly. First I will read the word, then the word within the sentence in your test, then I will repeat the word a third time.*

You should now read the spellings three times, as given below. Leave at least a 12-second gap between spellings. At the end, read all the sentences again, giving your child the chance to make any changes they wish to their answers.

| Question | Spelling | Marks |
|---|---|---|
| **Test 1** | | |
| 1 | The word is **accident**. *An **accident** closed the road.* The word is **accident**. | 1 |
| 2 | The word is **disagree**. *He had to **disagree** with the reporter.* The word is **disagree**. | 1 |
| 3 | The word is **finally**. *They **finally** announced the winner.* The word is **finally**. | 1 |
| 4 | The word is **science**. *I like doing experiments in **science** lessons.* The word is **science**. | 1 |
| 5 | The word is **considerable**. *They had a **considerable** wait for their lunch.* The word is **considerable**. | 1 |
| 6 | The word is **doubt**. *I had no **doubt** who had made the mess.* The word is **doubt**. | 1 |
| 7 | The word is **tremendous**. *The applause at the end was **tremendous**.* The word is **tremendous**. | 1 |
| 8 | The word is **treasure**. *The children found **treasure** at the end of the hunt.* The word is **treasure**. | 1 |
| **Test 2** | | |
| 1 | The word is **decision**. *The **decision** to stop the race was unpopular.* The word is **decision**. | 1 |
| 2 | The word is **forgetting**. *James was always **forgetting** his bag.* The word is **forgetting**. | 1 |
| 3 | The word is **preparation**. *There was a lot of **preparation** to do for the show.* The word is **preparation**. | 1 |
| 4 | The word is **chef**. *The **chef** was cooking lunch for the group.* The word is **chef**. | 1 |
| 5 | The word is **essential**. *It is **essential** that you listen to instructions.* The word is **essential**. | 1 |
| 6 | The word is **ought**. *They **ought** to take an umbrella with them.* The word is **ought**. | 1 |
| 7 | The word is **cautious**. *It is a good idea to be **cautious** when you try things for the first time.* The word is **cautious**. | 1 |
| 8 | The word is **aisle**. *The bride walked down the **aisle** on her wedding day.* The word is **aisle**. | 1 |
| **Test 3** | | |
| 1 | The word is **mystery**. *It was a **mystery** that needed to be solved.* The word is **mystery**. | 1 |
| 2 | The word is **young**. *It is fun to be **young** and adventurous!* The word is **young**. | 1 |
| 3 | The word is **musician**. *The **musician** played to a full concert hall.* The word is **musician**. | 1 |
| 4 | The word is **chorus**. *All the children were able to join in with the **chorus** of the song.* The word is **chorus**. | 1 |
| 5 | The word is **league**. *The football club was top of the **league**.* The word is **league**. | 1 |
| 6 | The word is **deceive**. *The magician was able to **deceive** his audience.* The word is **deceive**. | 1 |
| 7 | The word is **transferred**. *The goods were **transferred** from the lorry to the ship.* The word is **transferred**. | 1 |
| 8 | The word is **hesitant**. *The police officer was **hesitant** to make an arrest in case it was the wrong person.* The word is **hesitant**. | 1 |

You have completed all the tests! Now write your scores in the score chart below.

| Test | My Score |
|------|----------|
| Test 1 | /12 |
| Test 2 | /12 |
| Test 3 | /10 |
| Test 4 | /11 |
| Test 5 | /11 |
| Test 6 | /10 |
| Test 7 | /10 |
| Test 8 | /10 |
| Test 9 | /10 |
| Test 10 | /10 |
| Test 11 | /10 |
| Test 12 | /10 |
| Test 13 | /10 |
| Test 14 | /10 |
| Spelling Test 1 | /8 |
| Spelling Test 2 | /8 |
| Spelling Test 3 | /8 |
| **Total** | **/170** |

## How did you do?

**I did brilliantly!**
Fabulous!

**I did well.**
Great stuff!

**I did ok.**
Well done – keep up the practice if you want to improve.

**I didn't do so well.**
Don't worry – there's still time to learn and practise. Why not try these tests again?